I Can

Ace My College Interview

by Ashley Schmitt

Table of Contents

Chapter 1

What Will I Get
Out of this Book?

You may be asking yourself "Why should I read this book?" "What will I get out of it?" This book was designed with you, a high school student, in mind. The writing is straight forward, easy to read, without filler or fluff, and packed with lots of examples that are based on real students' experiences. The methods taught in this book are simple to understand and are very effective with practice.

I based this book on my experience working as a Regional Director of Admissions at a prestigious university and my work in preparing students for multiple college interviews. I have reviewed thousands upon thousands of student files for admissions, and I hate to say it, but many of the applications began to look very much alike. Amazing students, like yourself, become no more than a name in a file. After reading thousands of files you start to see what sets students apart. Grades and activities help, but many students have very similar grades and activities. No, what sets students apart is if they can tell stories that connect with the Admissions Officers and offer real insight into the student's mind and life. The best way to accomplish this is through the interview.

As I work with students, it absolutely amazes me how much a student can improve on their interview skills. In the beginning, some students can barely answer "tell me about yourself" in a concise manner. But after being taught a structured interview method, some coaching, and practice, the student is able dazzle an interviewer. The difference really is night and day. The student goes from awkward and dull, to eloquent and very interesting. After applying the techniques and methods taught in this book, it is completely possible for you to improve your interview skills. Believe me, it will impress your interviewer when he speaks with a fascinating, well-spoken, and confident individual, you.

I want to emphasize that being interesting and fascinating does not mean that you must have traveled the world, baked a two-story tall cupcake, been on television, or anything crazy. People are ALL fascinating, it is the little details about our lives that make us unique and interesting to others. In broad sweeps many of us sound or appear alike. For example, you can group students by SAT/ACTs and grades. Those within certain ranges have very similar profiles, similar scores, similar grades, and many times the same activities. That is what Admissions Officers see. They see a set of students within a certain range. The broad stroke approach makes all the students look the same. As an Admissions Officer, I knew they were not the same. I would dig a little deeper and look for interesting details that made the person unique.

I found that many students only gave vague details with no interest or color. I was able to pull very little out that seemed different. Some students were the exception. They gave me colorful stories and insight into how and why they thought a certain way. These were the students who stood out to me. The students whose files I carefully read and made sure to consider for admission. The details matter. They can make a difference.

The stories about you and your life matter. They make you the unique person you are. This book was written to help you search inside yourself for the details. Once you have gathered the stories that make up your life, this book will teach you an easy to learn method to express who you are to an interviewer. This book will help you tell the stories about your life that make Admissions Officers remember you and seriously consider you as a candidate for your chosen university.

As a prospective college student you will also need to write several college essays. Look for my book I Can Write An Extraordinary College Essay on Amazon. It teaches techniques similar to this book and will help you write essay that will stand out from the crowd.

Good Luck!

Chapter 2

Fair Warning

If only it was that easy

I will give you fair warning. Just reading this book WILL NOT help you have a great interview. You MUST be willing to put the work in and apply the techniques. This is not a long book, but there brainstorming activities and action items at the end of the Great Answers to the Most Common Questions Chapter. DO THEM. Interviewing is a skill and like any skill it must be learned and then PRACTICED until it becomes natural and an integrated part of your skill set. I have taught many students these skills and only with practice have they improved. I promise if you learn the techniques I teach and work to apply them, your interview skills will improve dramatically. You can and will shine during any interview. You will feel prepared and wonder why anyone feels that interviews are difficult.

Consider this line of thinking. If you want to go to any big university, you get good grades and take Honors Courses, AP/IB Courses, or other Advanced Courses. So, let me ask a question. Would you ever go into your Math class on test day without learning the material, taking notes, or reviewing any of the teacher's examples? Would you go in blind and hope for an A? No, you would not. That would be stupid, right? You take notes in class, do your homework, and at least the night before the test review your homework and notes.

Interviews are the same as a Math test, it is not something you just "know" how to do. You have to put in the work, practice (do your homework) and review right before the big day. So, put in the work and dazzle those interviewing you!

Chapter 3

Stand In Your Interviewer's Shoes

Since your resumes are all the same, we'll play musical chairs to see who gets in.

The purpose of an interview is to see who you really are. A person cannot be reduced to a transcript, resume, and an essay or two. People are far more interesting and complex than that. The interview is a chance for the interviewer to see beyond your academic scores and beyond the list of activities on a piece of paper. You need to come alive to them. You need to be a three-dimensional person with interesting stories and human depth. If done correctly, the interview is a chance for you to stand out from the crowd.

An interview is a very effective tool for people to decide who the best of the best is, and who really stands head and shoulders above the rest. The interview is considered an excellent discriminator. Now, put yourself in the shoes of the interviewers. They are trying to pick who should attend the college from a list of students. Those interviewing have all the resumes, essays and transcripts. Everybody has good a GPA. Everyone has good SAT scores and ACT scores. Everyone has a huge list of activities. Over half are Captain of some sports team. The other half is on the short list for valedictorian. Some are sports team Captains and valedictorians. The completion is fierce.

Unfortunately, this mass group of students with grades, test scores, and various honors looks very similar. You look like everyone else on paper. But you are NOT like everyone else.

You are unique, interesting, and most of all you REALLY want to go to the university or college of your choice. So, how can you stand out? The interview! It is one of the tools used to make the deciding choice. So, you need to impress the interviewer.

In any interview think about the person interviewing you and what they want to see. Most universities and colleges are interested in seeing that a student has acceptable/good grades and participates in a variety of activities. They are looking for examples of leadership, character, and being able to think through problems. They want to see that you participate in more than just academics, but in various activities like sports, music, clubs and community involvement.

I tend to generalize what interviewers are looking for into the categories below.

Leadership: The interviewer wants to see examples that depict your problem solving skills, ability to take and give direction, and ability to work with a variety of people.

Character: The interviewer wants to see examples of integrity. Examples that show you have solid integrity under pressure. (This is especially true for colleges who pride themselves on their honor code.)

Participation in a variety of activities: The interviewer wants to see examples that you participate in a variety of school activities like sports, clubs, choir, band, and school leadership. The interviewer wants examples of community involvement, such as church, volunteer work, community activities, recreational sports, and work experience. College is more than an academic experience it is a complete learning experience to include all the social and interaction experiences. An interviewer wants to see that you will enhance the campus and work with others around you. An interviewer does not expect that you have participated in all the listed activities. Instead they are looking to see you have participated in a variety of things from each of these categories. Variety is the key word. Not just sports, not just school clubs, and not just volunteer work.

True interest in the university: The interviewer wants to see examples that you have a real interest in university. You need to know something about the university and why you want to go there.

Did you notice anything similar across those three categories? EXAMPLES. Yes they want to see examples. There is a catch though. Remember to see your interview through the eyes of the person interviewing you. The interviewer has your resume. If you offer your examples as a huge list, you are not adding anything they did not already know about you. Examples, in an interview, are stories or antidotes about you and your involvement in leadership, character, activities, and knowledge about the college.

They want to know about you. They want to know details that make you different from everybody else. Example stories give you life and give you a third dimension that other students will not have. They want to be able to decide if you are someone who will be able to handle the challenging social and academic environment of the college. College is sometime stressful and academically demanding. They need to know whomever they pick will be able to handle those stresses, succeed and make the campus a more interesting/better place. They are trying to determine if you will be able to organize your time and juggle multiple activities. You need to think from that point of view as you create your examples. The interviewer will determine what type of person you are based on your past performance. The better and more detailed your stories, the better they can predict your future success.

To do this you need to brag about yourself through your example stories. But flat out bragging can come across as rude or hard to listen to. You probably know someone that you hate to be around because all they do is talk about how wonderful they are. There is a fine line between bragging and showing those interviewing you that you will succeed. Here is the essence of annoying bragging, "I can do this and this and this….." No examples and no engaging story. But there is an acceptable way to brag. The method is called STAR stories. A STAR story offers a way to brag about yourself that sounds very acceptable to people because it comes across as interesting and engages people through the story. Very succinctly, you tell people what you have accomplished in your life and offer results from your actions. The interviewer can then judge for themselves, from your actions and results, if what you accomplished was amazing or not. The STAR story method helps you tell them about yourself in a manner that comes across as very factual and very interesting. You are not bragging at that point of time. You are telling them about yourself and it really excites an interviewer to hear about students doing amazing things.

Chapter 4
Your Key to Success

"What a brilliant idea!"

The way to dazzle your interviewer is by learning a simple, yet very effective method to answer questions. STAR stories are your key to a successful interview. I promise you that if you put in the work to craft excellent STAR stories that your interviews will stand head and shoulders above everyone else's interview.

STAR
S: Situation
T: Task
A: Action
R: Result or Results

This method is an extremely effective way to frame the experiences in your life and to tell interviewers about your life and your experiences. Each part of the STAR acronym is important, but the last two (your actions, your results) are probably the most important and where you should spend the most time explaining. I want to highlight one other item. This is a STAR story not a STAR list. You want to create a story, create something memorable. Most students and actually most adults when asked any question about themselves start to list a bunch of qualities. This is not very interesting or does it tell the interviewer anything new. You need to create a story that shows the interviewer what type of person you are.

So, how do you create a STAR story? Take events in your life where you have accomplished something, lead an activity, helped someone, saw someone compromising their integrity, got through a difficult time in your life, solved a challenging problem, or confronted a teacher or coach on an issue that meant a lot to you. There is a brainstorming exercise later, but let's start by thinking about a time you lead an event or a group of people. It does not matter if you were the formal leader or if it was in school, sports, or in the community. Got an event in mind? Start with the S, write down a few thoughts and repeat for each letter of STAR.

Here are a few examples.

Example 1

The Junior Class organizes prom (Situation) and I was in charge of decorations (Task). I recruited a committee of other students and a teacher as a supervisor. I made sure to create an agenda and we met weekly. At our meetings, I encouraged participation from the group and assigned each member tasks. At the meetings we shared our progress and helped each other with anything not completed. I made sure to update our teacher of our progress and discussed what she could do to help us (Action). As a result of our organization and work together attitude the prom decorations were the best our school had seen and had come $100 under budget (Results).

Comments: The situation and task were kept short and gave just enough information to give the listener context. The list of actions accomplished was specific to what the speaker actually did. If the speaker had simply stated "I organized the committee to get the decorations done" the listener would not have any true detail to what the speaker had done. Notice the verbs used; recruited, created, encouraged, shared, discussed, updated. Verbs tell actions. Use verbs to describe the actions. The results were clear; saved $100 and best decorations seen.

Example 2

I was the Co-Chair on my church's youth committee. Our committee was in charge of organizing and executing all activities for the Youth Adventure Weekend. A 3-night 4-day campout for over 300 youth (Situation). As Co-Chair I needed to provide an overarching theme, create sub-committees, and insure everything was done (Task). I knew I wanted the event to be very special, so I spent days gathering information on what other groups had done from across the country. I gathered what I thought where the best activities. My theme was "The Lord will lead the way". I created a presentation that laid out all the activities and skits that would introduce each activity. I discussed with my Co-Chair who was thrilled I had a plan. We both presented the information to the rest of the youth committee and gained support from all. Everyone commented and the Youth Adventure Weekend was tweaked so all were excited. I assigned tasks, created sub-committees, and followed up on each (Action). The day of the event came and we were all prepared. I was thrilled when the adult leadership commented on how proud they were of me, my committee, and how well the event turned out (Results).

Comments: The situation and task were longer in this example but the speaker tried to give enough information so the listener could follow. Also, the length of the event and the numbers of youth were mentioned so the listener could understand the size of event planned. An event for 10 people is much different than a several day, overnight event for 300. The actions section contained several verbs to describe all the happened. The results discussed included that everything was prepared and ready for the event. Also, the results include comments that the adults were very happy with the speaker and the committee for the positive results.

Example 3

I was watching the news with my parents and saw that a tornado had completely destroyed a small town in Oklahoma. The screen showed a tiny girl holding her mom and crying. The family had nothing, and I felt that I had to do something to help (Situation). The picture of the little girl really spoke to me. I decided that I would help the kids in the town by collecting teddy bears to make them feel better (Task). I started by asking my parents for help. They agreed to ask around at work for teddy bears and donations. Next, I called my church and asked to put in an announcement in the bulletin that Sunday to ask for donations. Last, I went to school and spoke with our Service League and asked how they could help. They offered to support a Teddy Bear Drive one Saturday at the local Mall. My parents and I collected the money and bears as they came in (Action). Before, I knew it our garage was filled with just over 2,000 teddy bears. With the help of the monetary donations and a few corporate sponsors we were able to ship all the bears to the town in Oklahoma. I will always treasure the thank you note and photo that came back showing kids with the bears (Results).

Comments: This is an excellent example of leadership. The speaker was not called as a formal leader for school or the community, instead she saw a need and formed a plan to fill the need. The actions clearly showed how the student rallied the community to help and it resulted in 2,000 teddy bears to kids in need. Remember you do not need to actually be a leader or a captain of a team to show leadership. You just need to step up and lead.

Example 4

I spent my summers mowing lawns in my neighborhood for extra spending money. One day an older gentleman, Mr. Smith, told that he was unable to pay me anymore and that I didn't need to mow his lawn again. About two weeks later, I was mowing across the street, and noticed Mr. Smith struggling to get his mower started (Situation/Task). I liked him and wanted to help him out. I knew he would have trouble pushing his old mower, even if he got it started. I told Mr. Smith to put his mower away, and I would handle the lawn. He protested. I explained that I would be happy to mow the lawn for free. I came back each week and mowed Mr. Smith's lawn. He couldn't pay me, but he would always bring me a root beer or lemonade (Action). At the end of the summer, Mr. Smith came by our house and spoke with my parents. He told them I had been mowing his lawn for free and that they had a wonderful son who they should be very proud of. I was embarrassed, but my parents were proud that I had helped Mr. Smith. I learned that service means a great deal to the people we help (Results).

Comments: In this example the Situation and Task were combined. The speaker's actions were very clear. He decided to help his neighbor by mowing the lawn even though he was not going to get paid. The results were a simple thank you and the speaker stated what he learned about service. This is an excellent STAR story about character. It is easy for someone to say they have good character, but this example SHOWS good character. If asked about your community service or your character, think about a time you have served someone and tell the story. It does not have to be a major event. It can be something small that you noticed and just decided to help. Your actions will give those interviewing you a very clear picture of what kind of person you are.

Example 5

I work at a sandwich shop a few evenings a week and on weekend. My job is to make the sandwiches and clean the tables. One evening, the night manager and I were cleaning up and getting ready to go home. I noticed that he took some of the money from the cash register out and separated it from the rest before he brought the drawer back to the safe in the back. This seemed odd, but I wasn't sure if he had to count it a special way or needed it separate for some reason. A few nights later, I saw him take the small amount he had separated and slip it into his pocket before heading back (Situation/Task). I knew that this wasn't right. I decided to talk to the owner of the shop. I came in early the next day to talk to him. I told him what I saw and kept to the facts without accusing the night manager of anything. I felt that the owner should look into it (Action). A few weeks later, I had a new night manager. The owner came in that evening and thanked me for speaking up about what I saw. Apparently, the old manager had been stealing small amounts for a while. Without my input, the owner would have never caught him (Results).

Comments: In this example the student demonstrates his integrity. He stated what he saw and that he knew he should speak to the owner. This resulted in the owner finding out that someone was stealing from the cash register. Have you ever seen something that you knew didn't seem right? Did you tell someone? If so then you have an excellent STAR story about integrity. Even if you didn't tell anyone you can still use it as a good STAR story.

Think back to the event. What did you learn? What would you do now? If you had to do it over, would you tell someone? Why? The answers to these questions could be your result. Example: You saw someone cheating, but you didn't tell the teacher. To this day you still feel bad about not saying anything even though the event happened two years ago. You know now that you would say something because your conscience won't let another cheating incident like that go by without saying something. Show that you have learned and that you will do the right thing the next time.

Each example contained a story with the pertinent details. Details were specific to the situation and what was accomplished. You want to add color and life to your stories. If you have taken a writing course you will know that writing involves details. It is not just a tissue, it is a Kleenex. If talking about a car, it is not just a car. It is a Ford Mustang. You want the story to be succinct and no more than about a few minutes. To do that you need to offer vivid details that create a picture. Take the example of the car from above. If I said that I drove a car, what do you picture? Some vague car shaped object or maybe your favorite car. Each interviewer might picture something different. If I said I drove a red Ford Mustang everyone has pretty much the same picture in their head.

Adding specific, vivid details helps the interviewer see the same picture. The trick is to decide what details are really important to the story. Too much detail can make a story drag on too long. In Example 2 the speaker included the detail about 300 youth attending the event. This definitely gives you a picture of how large the event was so it was an important detail. The detail stating the theme probably is not very important and could be left out. It is short though and adds some detail, but if a shorter answer is needed it could be left out. Look at the details of your story and make sure each offers substance to the story.

An important item to discuss about STAR stories is the results. Numbers, dollar figures, time saved or number of people led are very important to state in each STAR story. In fact, results are probably the most important part. Students usually leave out results whenever they are asked about their actions or activities. If you want to differentiate yourself from the other candidates adding the results of your actions will set you apart. In the above examples the results discussed were about dollars being saved, compliments from observers, number of teddy bears shipped, and lessons learned. The more specific the results the better, but stating that an event went well, with no problems, IS a result and should be stated if that is all you can think of. If an event didn't go well, state what you learned and how you would fix it the next time.

Brainstorming STAR stories

I have an activity for you to complete at the end of this section that will help brainstorm STAR stories. With it I want you to come up with eight or nine ideas for STAR stories. If you could come up with more, great! But at least eight or nine. You will use the generated ideas in Chapter 5: Great Answers to the Most Common Questions.

You need to vary the examples throughout your life. Do not pull every example from sports. Do not pull every example from academics. Provide examples from several of your activities. For example, one about academics, one about sports, one about leadership in your church, one about school involvement, one about a community activity, and one about a club. Pick examples from all over your life.

Brainstorming Activity

IMPORTANT: The purpose of this activity is to get you thinking. Look at each word and ask yourself if you can think of ANY examples, unique stories, or thoughts you can associate with that word. If you think of something, jot a note down or circle the word. As you go through the list you will notice that certain activities or stories will come up several times. Those ones are most likely good STAR stories. Write the ideas and thoughts down for later use. You can use the ideas generated for the Chapter 5: Great Answers to the Most Common Questions. If you come up with extra that is great, but make sure to come up with eight or nine in total.

LIST

Adapted (teaching styles/special tools)
Administered (programs)
Advised (people/peers/job-seekers)
Analyzed (data/blueprints/schematics/policies)
Appraised (services/value)
Arranged (meetings/events/training programs)
Assembled (automobiles/computers/apparatus)

Audited (financial records/accounts payable)
Budgeted (expenses)
Calculated (numerical data/annual costs/mileage)
Cataloged (art collection/technical publications)
Checked (accuracy/other's work)
Classified (documents/plants/animals)
Cleaned (houses/auto parts)
Coached (teams/students/athletes)
Collected (money/survey information/data/samples)
Compiled (statistics/survey data)
Confronted (people/difficult issues)
Constructed (buildings)
Consulted (on new designs/investment strategy)
Coordinated (events/work schedules)
Corresponded (with other departments/colleagues)
Counseled (students/peers/job-seekers)
Created (new programs/artwork/internet sites)
Cut (diamonds/concrete/fabric/glass/lumber)
Decided (which equipment to buy/priorities)
Delegated (authority)
Designed (data systems/greeting cards)
Directed (administrative staff/theatre productions)
Dispensed (medication/information)
Displayed (results/products/artifacts)
Distributed (products/mail)
Dramatized (ideas/problems/plays)
Edited (publications/video tape/)
Entertained (people)
Established (objectives/guidelines/policies)
Estimated (physical space/costs/staffing needs)
Evaluated (programs/instructors/peers/students)
Exhibited (plans/public displays/evidence)
Expressed (interest in development projects)
Facilitated (multimedia exhibit/conflict resolution)
Found (missing persons/appropriate housing)
Framed (houses/pictures)
Generated (interest/support)
Grew (plants/vegetables/flowers)
Handled (detailed work/data/complaints/toxins)

Hosted (panel discussions/foreign students)
Implemented (registration system/new programs)
Improved (maintenance schedule/systems)
Initiated (production/changes/improvements)
Inspected (physical objects/repairs/electrical work)
Installed (software/bathrooms/electrical systems/parts)
Interpreted (languages/new laws/schematics/codes)
Interviewed (people/new employees)
Invented (new ideas/machine parts)
Investigated (problems/violations/fraud)
Landscaped (gardens/public parks/indoor gardens)
Led (foreign tours/campus tours)
Listened (to others/to conference calls)
Located (missing information/facilities)
Maintained (transportation fleet/aircraft/diesel engines)
Managed (an organization/a mail room/a retail store)
Measured (boundaries/property lines/bridge clearance)
Mediated (between people/civil settlements)
Met (with dignitaries/public/community groups)
Monitored (progress of others/water flow/electric usage)
Motivated (workers/trainees)
Negotiated (contracts/sales/labor disputes)
Operated (equipment/hydraulic test stand/robotics equipment)
Organized (tasks/library books/data bases)
Painted (houses/cars/aircraft/interiors)
Patrolled (runways/public places/property/buildings)
Persuaded (others/customers)
Planned (agendas/international conferences)
Predicted (future needs/stock market trends)
Presented (major selling points/new products)
Prepared (reports/meals/presentations)
Printed (books/reports/posters)
Processed (human interactions)
Programmed (computers)
Promoted (events/new products/new technology)
Proofread (news/reports/training materials)
Protected (property/people)
Published (reports/books/software)
Purchased (equipment/supplies/services)

Questioned (people/survey participants/suspects/witnesses)
Raised (performance standards/capital investments)
Read (volumes of material/news releases)
Recorded (data/sales totals/music/video)
Recruited (people for hire/executives/Marines)
Rehabilitated (people/old buildings)
Repaired (mechanical devices/exhaust systems)
Reported (findings/monthly activity)
Researched (library documents/cancer/diseases)
Renewed (programs/contracts/insurance policies)
Reviewed (program objectives/books and movies)
Revised (instructional materials)
Scheduled (social events/doctor's appointments)
Sold (advertising space/real estate/cars)
Served (individuals)
Sewed (parachutes/clothing/upholstery)
Signed (for the hearing impaired)
Sketched (charts and diagrams)
Spoke (in public)
Supervised (others)
Taught (classes/math/science)
Tailored (clothing/services)
Televised (conferences/training/events/shows)
Tested (new designs/students/employees)
Updated (files)
Verified (reports/identity)
Volunteered (services/time)
Wrote (reports/training manuals)
Weighed (trucks/patients/precious metals)
Welded (bike frames/airframes/alloys)
X-rayed (limbs/stressed equipment)

Chapter 5

Great Answers to the Most Common Questions

"I only have one question for applicants:
Does or does not 1 + 1 = 2?"

Yes, there are questions that your interviewer will probably ask. So, be prepared for them. Coming across as interesting and confident is a mixture of preparation and practice. This chapter will walk you through some of the most commonly asked questions during an interview. First, the question is stated with some commentary on what the interviewer is looking for and the mindset for the question. Next, are some suggestions on how to answer the question. Then, there will be an example answer to the question based on the experiences of real teenagers. I do want to stress that this is an example answer. You need to come up with your own, based on your OWN life. But I am a huge fan of examples, so each question has an example answer for you. After the example are comments about the example pointing out various thoughts or ideas. Last, is the Action Items. The Action Items are a list of your to dos for each question. The Action Items will prompt you on how to start forming your own answer to the question.

A few tips when forming your answers.

1) Always try to be positive. Even if the experience is negative try to look at the most positive aspects, such as what you have learned.

2) Take some time to think about your answers. Try not to use the first example that pops into your head. See if there are other possibilities or answers.

3) This is NOT easy. Give yourself a break. You are learning a new skill and that just takes time and effort. If you get frustrated, take a break, and then get back to work.

4) Remember to include the details about your experiences. Before you create your answer think about the sights, sounds, and smells of the incident. It might help you recreate it for the interviewer.

Tell Me About Yourself

This seems an easy question and many students just answer it without thought. That is a huge mistake! All interview questions offer you a chance to shine and become more than a name on a resume. You should translate this question to "Show me something interesting about yourself that I do not already know from your resume or essay(s)." There are two key points for this question: 1) "Show" the interviewer something 2) it needs to be new and unique to you.

This is a question you should take some serious consideration before you answer. Otherwise you will answer with a common descriptor like determined, a good student, hard worker, motivated, or a laundry list of your activities. Admissions Officers have heard every basic description out there. You want to show the Admissions Officer what is interesting and unique about you. Many suggest you come up with something truly off-the-wall so that the interviewer remembers you. Things like you once baked an enormous world record pie or you love to go skydiving with your dog.

While I agree that you want the interviewer to remember you, I feel you are better off "showing" how you are unique and different in a manner that reflects your character, leadership, or personality. If you have an off-the-wall example, work with it to make sure you show your positive qualities rather than just a "gimmick" to help you be remembered.

Start by brainstorming a few things you love to do. Then ask yourself what are your great character, leadership or personal qualities? Which activity exemplifies one or two of those qualities? Create a STAR story with that activity to show your passion and unique traits to the interviewer. Offer the interviewer your list of a few things you love to and then state your STAR story.

Example
Tell me about yourself.

I really enjoy reading, writing short stories, being on the swim team, and I'm very passionate about tutoring younger students in Algebra. I have one student, Sarah, who is an amazing artist, but math is extremely difficult for her. In fact she was getting an F in class. Her parents insisted she pass Algebra before she was allowed to take an advanced art class (Situation). It was my job to make sure she did (Task). At first, I was worried. I went over every assignment and class example. She just couldn't understand how to do the problems. I did not want to give up and was determined to help her. She was really trying, but just couldn't seem to connect the concepts. I took a step back and tried to see what parts she was understanding. I started to build upon those concepts and created a different method of explaining each problem. I wrote out the step-by-step instructions for my method and then let her try the problems (Action). To both her and my delight she was able to do most of the problems without my help! Once, I figured out how to teach her there was no stopping our progress. It was the best feeling to see her proudly holding her report card with a C. She was thrilled she passed and was able to take her art class (Result).

Comments: The list of activities included two academic items, one sports, and one volunteer activity. Pick a variety of activities, not just from one part of your life, but from several. Now, what qualities did the speaker "show" to the interviewer? How about determination, a willingness to help someone, problem-solving skills, creation of a new teaching method, patience, and probably a few other things. That is the beauty of a STAR story! A well-crafted story, with details that make the story come alive, demonstrates a wide variety of your best qualities.

Action Items

- Brainstorm 3-4 things you love to do.
- What great qualities do you have?

- Which one of those activities highlights one or two of those qualities?
- Formulate a STAR story to show the interview who you are.
- Practice your answer and STAR story!

Why Are You Interested in Attending (Enter College Name Here)?

Translate this to, "What about our college specifically interests you?" Specifically, that is the key word. An interviewer wants to know that you have done research and picked that college for a precise reason.

Answers such as:
My parents/friends/counselor want me to go here.
I can make a lot of money if I graduate from here.
I'm only here for the soccer scholarship.
You are my second choice school.
This school is close to home.

Are not exactly what an interviewer would like to hear. Some or all of those reasons might be true, but you should spend a little time researching the school for other reasons. You are going to spend the next four years there. You should put a little thought into what about the college, campus, or its activities might interest you. Start by getting on the school's website and doing some research. Look at your potential majors' webpages. What about each interests you academically? Look at the college's events calendar for the past year. What activities, talks, rallies, or other events interest you? If you live close, take a walking tour. See what is going on around campus. See what the atmosphere feels like and look at the various common areas where events are posted. Once you have done this come up with an academic reason you would like to go there and one or two specific extra activities you are interested in. Remember be specific!

Example

Why Are You Interested in Attending (Enter College Name Here)?

I am considering majoring in history. I know that the History Department is considered one of the best in the State. I saw that Professor Smith just won an award for his journal article about George Washington. Washington is one of my favorite people in history. I think I would find a good fit in that department. Also, I noticed that the campus has a club that does historical reenactments. When I was young my father did those. I would really like to join the club and try doing a few reenactments. It seems like it would be fun and it ties to my interest in history.

Comments: The key to this is that the student told specifically what interested him. He mentioned a professor who had just won an award and then explained his interest in that subject matter. The interviewer knows that the student has done some research and has really thought about why he wants to go to the college. Also, the student mentions a club and his interest in a specific activity. Take some time to decide why you want to go to the college and then pull out specific details to support your answer.

Action Items

- Look at the webpages of your potential majors.
- What interests you about each?
- Is there any awards or articles about the departments you can relate to?
- Take a look at the Events Calendar for the past year.
- What would you like to participate in?
- If you are close by take a walking tour.
- What is the atmosphere? Any events going on that interest you?
- Find an academic reason and 1 or 2 extracurricular reasons to go to the college.
- Practice your answer!

Tell Me About a Challenge in Your Life.

Life is full of challenges. It is what you do with those challenges that define you and make you who are. College is full of challenges, too. Choices to be made and times when things are difficult. Each challenge you overcome gives you the experience you need to solve your next problem.

An interview is about getting to know you and in this question the interviewer wants to know if you can think through a situation and solve a problem. What problems have you overcome that will let you solve your next problem? Let's start to think of the question from that point of view. Think about a time you had to come up with a plan to solve a problem. You are most likely very proud of yourself for solving this problem. Or you feel you learned a great deal from the experience.

The problem does not need to be life threatening or extremely personal. (Try to avoid being overly personal and making your interviewer uncomfortable.) Did you find a way to pass Calculus? Did you resolve a dispute with a teacher, student, or boss that was difficult to deal with? Did you work to overcome an injury and win the big competition? Did you start a charity in honor of a lost friend or family member? Did you find a way to do the right thing when you were pressured to cheat or steal?

Once you have an event in mind, begin to think about the events that led up to the problem. Think about how you initially reacted. Think about what happened as you began to gather information about the problem. What step-by-step actions did you take to solve the problem? What happened after? Now, write your STAR story.

Example

Tell Me About a Challenge in Your Life.

I was the President of my High School's Service Club. We had a "Clean Up the City Parks" service project coming up in about a month (Situation). Last year, the event had not gone well due to poor attendance, organization and people getting lost. I decided we could do better and began to create a plan (Task). Unfortunately, the teacher who oversaw our club e-mailed out a list of the teams without speaking to me. This is what we had done the year before and it had not gone well. No true consideration had gone into the team list and we weren't even sure if the people on the list could attend. It meant some parks had many people to help and others only had one or two.

I was upset, but I decided that I needed to be able to work with this teacher the rest of the year. I asked if we could talk after school about the event. When we spoke, I politely explained a few of the problems we had last year and that I thought I had a way to avoid a few of them. Then, I showed him my plan. I had created a web-based sign-up tool that students could fill out. It limited the number of people at each location and made sure we would have enough people at each site. It also had a printable map and sent the information as a calendar invite once you signed up. My teacher was very impressed. He explained that we had not spoken much about the event and he didn't realize I had been working on something. He immediately sent out another e-mail and pointed people to the website (Action). I realized that I probably should have spoken to my teacher earlier. If we have talked, we would have avoided the conflicting e-mails. Fortunately, our Clean Up the City Parks went great and each park looked spotless after we got done (Results).

Comments: This is a great example of two challenging situations in one. First, the clean-up event the year before had not gone well. He knew he needed to overcome a failure from the previous year. Second, the teacher sent an e-mail out without consulting him about the event. The student was mad, but he controlled himself and went about solving his problem. This STAR story clearly showed the step-by-step method the student went about solving the problem. He spoke to his teacher and did so in a respectful manner. He then outlined the problems he saw from the previous year and demonstrated he had tried to fix them through a sign-up tool that provided reminders and maps. After talking with the teacher, he realized he had not been communicating with the teacher. The teacher's initial e-mail had been due to a lack of communication on the student's part. The student learned an important lesson AND the end result was that the event turned out much better than the year before.

Problem solving skills are essential in daily college life. Demonstrate your skills to the interviewer by showing them a time you solved a difficult problem or challenge.

Action Items

- Think about a time you solved a difficult problem.
- What events lead up to the problem?
- What were the step-by-step actions you took to solve the problem?
- What were the results?
- Formulate a STAR story.
- Practice your STAR story!

How can you contribute to the (Enter College Name Here) community?

Translate this question to "How can you enhance the "X" community?" Enhance means to make better, add to, or improve. Your grades, sparkling personality, ability to work hard, or sports prowess do not necessarily add to the community. This question is focused on looking outside yourself to what you can offer your fellow students and the academic institution itself. College is a life learning experience as much as an academic experience. How can you enhance the life learning experience of those around you?

Start by thinking about your hobbies and volunteer work. What two or three things do you enjoy doing? How can you help others with one or two of those things? What do you know about the college you are interviewing with and how can you apply your unique abilities? Maybe you have done something similar already in your high school or community.

Example: Let's say you enjoy being outdoors and camping. Is there a club that does that on campus? Do a quick internet search and find out. Let's say there is. You were able to take an intense week long survival class last summer and you are really excited to share what you learned with your fellow club members. If there isn't a club on campus, do you plan on starting a new club or finding others who might be interested in the survival skills you learned?

Once you have an idea of what you can contribute use the STAR story format as an outline to frame your response.

Example

How can you contribute to the (Enter College Name Here) community?

I am extremely passionate about running. I'm not fast or a state champion, but I love to run in 5k and 10k races all over the state. Last year, my aunt developed breast cancer (Situation). My mother, who also likes to run, suggested we enter a charity race to raise money for breast cancer research (Task). I agreed, and we spent the next three months asking friends, family, my mother's co-workers, church members, and students from my school to donate money or to join us in the race (Action). We had donations totally over $7,000. I would really enjoy organizing a group of students on campus, like the school's running club, to do a charity run and see how much we can raise for a good cause (Result).

Comments: In this example the student took one of her passions, running, and had already done something to enhance her community. She had done a charity run and with her mother's help raised $7,000. Then she stated that she would like to do something similar at the college. There are two things to point out in this STAR story. 1) The experience provides tangible proof that the student's ability to enhance the community is likely. She has already done it once in her own community, she can do it again. Past performance is an excellent indicator of future performance. 2) It hinted at the fact that the student is knowledgeable about the clubs on campus and is serious about attending.

Look at your passions and the volunteer work you have already done. What would you like to do in the future? Use one of your past successes to show that you WILL enhance the college community.

Action Items

- Brainstorm 2-3 things you love to do.
- How can you help others with one of those things? What have you done in the past to help people?
- Do a quick internet search on each college you are interviewing with to see if something like that already exists.
- If so, how can you contribute to it? If not, what can you do to start something or contribute to the community?

- Formulate a STAR story showing one of your past volunteer successes and how you would like to do something similar on campus.
- Practice the STAR story!

What do you like to do in your free time?

Translate this to "What productive thing do you like to do in your free time?" The interviewer is not interested in the fact you like to hang out with friends. Answering that you spend all your time studying isn't the right answer either. What interesting and productive things do you like to do? Remember that the interviewer is looking for students who will enhance the college atmosphere. So think of something fun, interesting, and productive. Do you like to play basketball at the park and organize games? Do you like to hike and last summer you and two friends accomplished a two-night trek out in the mountains? Did you take a CPR class and enjoy it so much that you became an instructor? Are you a running enthusiast and you have participated in four marathons in the past two years?

I agree that "fun" varies, depending on the person, but this is an interview about you. What do you find fun? I love to run, bike and swim. So, I trained for a year for a 70.3 mile triathlon race and was ecstatic that I was not last. What crazy thing do you love to do, and what did you learn about yourself or how did you help someone else?

Example

What do you like to do in your free time?

Recently, I have been helping my Mom with her class. She teaches special education and has a lot of kids who could use extra attention. At first, I did it because my Mom asked me to help her, but lately I have enjoyed it. The kids are really fun to work with and very kind. They have so much joy in them and they see the world in such a different way. High school and peer pressure is tough, but that doesn't touch these kids. They just want to share the simple joy of playing soccer or running a high-spirited race. There is this one kid, Jason. He and I have become buddies. I have been teaching him basketball. He loves it and is pretty good at throwing free-throw shots. I try to spend at least twice a week or more there. It brightens my day to see Jason and the other kids.

Comments: Helping others is a great example of something interesting, fun, and productive. This student started helping because of an obligation, but soon it became a joy to help. What activity of yours is a joy and meaningful to others. Or what crazy goal did you accomplish (like my triathlon)?

Action Items

- Brainstorm 3-4 things you love to do
- How have you helped others with one of those things?
- Or is one of them a crazy goal you accomplished?
- Create your story about the event(s).
- Practice your answer!

Tell me about a time you were a leader or displayed leadership?

Leadership is the art of getting a group of people to work together towards a common goal or objective. College is an interactive experience. There are group projects in academia and all the extras associated with campus life. Interviewers are interested in how you work with others and how you can help others achieve success

Think about times you acted as a leader of a group. An official title was not necessary. To be a leader all you had to do was to take actions that moved the group towards a common goal. Find two or three experiences in your life where you helped a group get to their goal. Which one of those do you feel was the most successful? What did you specifically do to make it successful? Draft a STAR story to highlight your actions.

Example
Tell me about a time you were a leader or displayed leadership?

Each summer I work for my Dad in his construction business (Situation). Normally, I just help the crews, move equipment around, and run errands. This past summer my Father gave me a challenge. He put me in charge of clearing and maintaining the mountainous dirt roads that went in and out of the site (Task). The summer rains tend to wash away the roads and create dangerous driving conditions for the big construction vehicles. The roads need constant care. It was a big job and Dad let me hire my own crew. I picked a few people from Dad's normal road crew and hired a few of my friends for the summer. I had to create work schedules and balance the experienced crew with my new hirers. I was in charge of making sure people took breaks and also that they did the work assigned. I found it very challenging to be the boss of my friends and even had to fire one of them. That was really difficult, but it had to be done.

The most challenging part was motivating the crew during the downpours of rain. We had to quickly sandbag some areas or the whole road would wash away. It was incredibly hard to lug heavy sandbags in the mud and cold rain. During those times I worked twice as hard to show the crew that it could be done and that we needed to save the road (Action). By the end of the summer, I had learned a lot about people, motivating them, and how hard it is to be the boss. I made mistakes and learned, but in the end my Father said that he was really proud of me. He felt I had done as well as his seasoned managers (Results).

Comments: In this example the speaker was a formal leader of a construction crew. He hired a crew, created schedules, and made sure the work assigned was done. He also found that sometimes a boss needs to fire people for not doing the work. Additionally, he worked hard to motivate his crew during tough times. He was ultimately successful. This is a great example of leadership. He took various actions to get the work done, but was challenged with his friend's misbehaver and keeping people motivated. In your leadership experience, think about what you did to make it successful. Also, think about what made it challenging. What did you do to overcome those challenges?

Action Items

- Brainstorm 2-3 times you acted as a leader.
- Which one of those do you feel had the greatest success?
- What did you specifically do to make it successful?
- What were the challenges? What did you do to overcome them?
- What were the results?
- Formulate a STAR story.
- Practice your STAR story!

What Are Your Strengths and Weaknesses?

This is in many ways similar to the "Tell me about yourself" question. The interviewer wants to learn a little bit more about you and get a glimpse at your self-awareness. The question sounds like you should offer a list of characteristics or qualities, but you need to add more than that to impress the interviewer. Both your strengths and weaknesses need to be shown to the interviewer. A list of them does not offer the interviewer anything interesting or unique.

Also, you need to articulate your weaknesses. Do not say you have none. That is untrue. Everyone has weaknesses. You just need to pose them to the interviewer in a positive manner and describe how you plan to minimize them.

Make a list of your positive and negative qualities. Pick your top three positive qualities and three of your least negative qualities. Think of an example of a time you demonstrated one or more of your positive qualities. Draft a short STAR story. Think of an example of when you demonstrated one or more of your negative qualities. What did you learn and how are you trying to improve? Draft a short STAR story.

Example

What Are Your Strengths and Weaknesses?

My strengths are that I am very optimistic, I have a deep need to do what is right, and I am tenacious. I had a huge project due at school. Everyone was complaining that there was too much to do and the deadline was too short (Situation/Task). I shrugged off the negativity and got to work. I tried to do a little bit every day. A few days before the project was due, I had several of my friends ask if they could copy my work. I told them no. I had worked hard and that would be cheating. I did offer to help them by showing them what books and websites were really helpful for research. They were mad that I wouldn't let them copy, but were grateful for the help I did offer (Actions). I turned the project in on time. I was glad that I hadn't waited until the last few days to start (Result).

My weaknesses--- I tend to babble when I am nervous. I have a hard time visualizing what the graphs are supposed to look in my current Math class. I really need to study extra and work hard to understand the material. Last, I tend to miss what is going on around me when I am thinking. I felt really bad the other day. I was thinking about one of my friends and a problem she was going through. I was walking into the mall and wasn't paying attention to what was going on around me (Situation/Task). I didn't realize there was a woman with a walker just behind me. I walked in and let the heavy door shut behind me. I heard a noise that pulled me out of my thoughts and turned around. She had gotten her walker caught in the door. I felt awful. I immediately grabbed the door and held it open for her. I apologized for letting the door slam. She smiled at me and told me it was alright (Actions). I still felt bad. I need to pay more attention and not get too lost in my thoughts, so something like this doesn't happen again (Results/Lesson).

Comments: These two short STAR stories told the interviewer much more than a list of qualities. They showed the interviewer a slice into the life of the speaker. The strength example showed the interviewer that the student worked hard, made a plan to finish her task, could resist peer pressure and had personal integrity, and was willing to offer a friend help. Her weaknesses displayed that the student was self-aware. The example weakness was not anything special or amazing it was just an occurrence in her daily life. But it offered the interviewer a look into her feelings, actions, and desires to do what was right. She even tried to make it right by opening the door and apologizing. We all make mistakes and have weaknesses. Just show the interviewer you know what your weaknesses are and are working to improve.

Action Items

- Brainstorm your positive and negative qualities.
- Pick your top 3 positive qualities and 3 of your least negative qualities.
- Create a short STAR story to show your positive qualities in action.
- Create a short STAR story to show how you are working to improve your negative qualities or a story to show what you have learned from a weakness.
- Practice your short STAR stories.

What do you want to major in?

I want to offer some very sound advice at this point in time. I realize you are young and may not have an exact idea of what you want to do with your life. But I want to point out that you are planning on dedicating the next four years to becoming something. Your time is valuable, shouldn't you spend some time soul searching about what you want to become? As you learn and grow you can change your course, but spend a little time on yourself and search your heart for a course direction. Think of yourself as a huge ocean liner crossing the vast Atlantic Ocean. If you did not have a destination in mind, do you think you would even make it across? You might wander with the currents and never get to dry land again. Pick your destination and aim at it. Course correct as necessary, but have a general stopping point in mind.

That being said, an interviewer will understand if you are unsure on your major. If you have several in mind state which ones you are interested in and why. Show your passion for an area of study or a few subjects. Think about what fascinates you about the subject.

For example let's say you are interested in English and Psychology. You love English because the written word fascinates you. Words on paper have the ability to influence people, broaden their horizons, make them think, or pull emotions from their souls. It is amazing what words can do. But you are also interested in Psychology because you like to understand how people think. People are intriguing. Each person's mind seems to work in a different way and you want to understand why. Take a few minutes to think about WHY you are interested in a particular subject.

If you have a specific major in mind express why you are interested in that particular subject. Also, do you homework on the college for that major. Read the webpage and some of the current events about the school. Sprinkle in a few of the events you have heard about that interest you and honestly express why you think they are interesting.

For example you want to be a Mechanical Engineer. You have always been interested in how things work. As a kid your mother would be furious at you because you took all your toys apart and sometimes you couldn't put them back together. You have read that the school participates in a robot warrior competition and you would love to participate in something like that.

In all cases, avoid saying you are interested in a major because you will make a lot of money or it will make you prestigious. Be honest, humble, and earnest. You are going to college to learn. So focus on why you want to learn about a specific subject. Making a lot of money is up to you after your college experience.

Action Items

- Brainstorm 2-3 subjects you want to major in. If you already know which one, great move on to the next item.
- What about that major(s) interests you?
- Why does it interest you?
- Is there an experience in your life you can share? (Like the student above who took apart all his toys.).
- Look at the college's webpage and the majors' webpages. See if there are any current events that interest you and you can tie into your answer.
- Practice your answer so you are prepared.

Where do see yourself in 10 years?

Do you know what you will be doing in 10 years? If so then you are better off than most adults. The interviewer does not expect you to have an exact idea or very specific plan, but they want to know you are thinking ahead. Much like the question about "What do you want to major in?" you should have a destination in mind. If you have two or three ideas of what you want to do that is fine. Answer the question honestly with the two or three ideas and then make sure to explain why.

Example
Where do you see yourself in 10 years?

My family owns a small fast food restaurant. We serve hamburgers, fries, and the greatest chocolate chip milkshakes you have ever had. During the summer, I work in various parts of the business. Last year my Dad let me do the bookwork and accounting. I really enjoyed working with the numbers and seeing how the business worked on paper. Based on that experience, I would like to study finance and business. I can see myself either being an accountant, or possibly starting my own small business, like my Dad. Both interest me currently, and I would like to take a few business and accounting classes to see which path I should chose.

Action Items

- What 1, 2, or 3 things can you see yourself doing?
- Why are you interested in each one?
- What in your life make you feel like each one fits you?
- Build those thoughts into a clear answer.
- Practice your answer.

Who has influenced you the most over your lifetime?

There are several versions of this question. Who is your hero? What is your favorite fictional character? Who do you admire most? Who do you admire most in history? The interviewer is not necessarily interested in who, instead they are more interested in why you admire them or what type of influence they have had over your life. You need to articulate the qualities or characteristics that you admire and how that has influenced you.

Start by identifying three or four qualities you admire most. What real person, fictional character, and historic individual exemplify one or two of those qualities?

Example

Who has influenced you the most over your lifetime?

When I was about five years old, I was at the grocery store with my Dad. I knew it was wrong to take anything from a store and my parents had told me not to take candy without paying for it. Then, I saw an opened box of candy with most of the candy spilled all over the floor. I thought, "Eating candy off the floor can't be stealing, right?" So, I took the candy off the floor, put it in my mouth, and started to eat. A few minutes later my Dad asked what I was eating (Situation/Task). I told him candy that I had found on the floor. He grabbed the box, took my arm, and marched me up to customer service. By this time, I was confused and a little scared. He asked to see the store manager. I got really scared and began to cry. I knew I had done something wrong, but I was not sure what.

My dad found the store manager. I looked at him with tears in my eyes. The store manager looked at me, looked at my dad, looked at me and then back to my dad. My dad said, "My daughter has something to tell you."

With quite a few tears, I choked out my story of taking the candy. I said I was so sorry for taking it. The store manager said, "Well what would you like to do, Sir?"

He said, "My daughter will pay for it. I will give her the money, and she will pay for it out of her allowance when she gets home."
The store manager thought that sounded fair. My dad gave him the money, and I took what was left of the candy home (Actions).

On that day, I learned a huge lesson about integrity. I was young, but I had never been so ashamed of myself or so embarrassed. I remember my dad had no qualms about taking me right up to the store manager and making me face what I had done. Integrity like that, is something I truly admire and when I was young I knew I wanted to aspire to that level of integrity. From that moment on, my dad was my hero. I knew I wanted to be like him (Results).

Comments: This example shows why Dad was the student's hero and weaves a vivid story of how profoundly the quality of integrity was ingrained in the student. No matter if your person is fictional, real, or from history, find the quality you admire most and create a STAR story that shows that characteristic in action.

Action Items

- Brainstorm 3-4 qualities you admire.
- Which 1 or 2 stand out?
- Identify a real person, a fictional character, and someone from history that displays the quality.
- What action or story about your real person, fictional character, and someone from history highlights that quality?
- Formulate a short STAR story for each.
- Practice your STAR story!

Does your high school record accurately reflect your effort and abilities?

This question offers you a chance to explain a low grade or bad semester. The real trick is to remain positive. Complaining or blaming others for your actions will reflect poorly on you and in most cases look worse than the grade itself. If you had real extenuating circumstances, like your mother was in the hospital and you had to take care of your siblings, then relay the facts to the interviewer without drama or negativity. Or if you just have difficulty with Algebra then state that. You took the subject, you had trouble, and you studied hard, but failed the first time. You took it again, worked twice as hard, and got a B-. The interviewer will respect you for your honest assessment that the subject was hard for you AND that you took it again and worked harder.

The important part is to remain positive and factual. Poor grades or events that led up to poor grades have emotional baggage. DO NOT let the interviewer see your emotional baggage. Start to become the adult you hope to be in college. Do not blame others. Figure out what went wrong and learn from it.

Example

Does your high school record accurately reflect your effort and abilities?

Yes and no. Most of the grades I am very proud of. I worked hard, but I had trouble with Algebra the first time I took it. I just couldn't seem to understand how to work the equations and I had real trouble with word problems. I failed the first time. I was forced to go to summer school and retake the class. I was upset at first. Who really wants to be at summer school? I decided to make the most of it, since I had to be there. I found that taking Algebra during summer school helped. I only had that one class and was able to focus on learning the material. I found a volunteer tutor at the library to help me as well. I am happy to say that I passed with a B the second time. I realized that in some areas, like Algebra, I need to ask for help as soon as I realize I don't understand the material. I think if I had asked for help sooner the first time, I might have passed.

Comments: Notice there is no blaming the teacher or other students, just an honest "I did not understand." He talked about retaking the subject and what things helped. Such as, focusing on the one subject and getting help. He finished his answer with what he learned. This type of honest answer gives the interviewer insight into the student's self-awareness. College is hard. You will have difficult subjects. The interviewer now knows that this student will go and ask for help before failing a class.

Action Items

- Any grades you are not proud of?
- What happened? What didn't you understand?
- Was there a real extenuating circumstance?
- What did you learn?
- Gather the facts, organize them into a succinct answer, and then relay what you learned.

If you could do one thing in high school differently, what would it be?

Like the question about your school record, the trick for this one is to remain positive. The easiest way to do this is to express to the interviewer something you were interested in but did not try. Is there a club you wanted to join, but did not have time for? Were you interested in drama, but have stage fright? Did you wish, like me, that you had taken Spanish instead of French? Think of something that you wanted to do, but just did not for some reason. Why? What did you learn about yourself?

Example
If you could do one thing in high school differently, what would it be?

I really wish I would have gone Bungee Jumping with my friends. For my friend's 17th birthday, she went Bungee Jumping and invited all of us to go with her. I was excited at first and got my Dad to sign the permission slip. The day came and as we drove up I saw the tower. NO WAY! I couldn't do it. I was really afraid. My friends all jumped, but not me. They were really supportive and didn't press me too much. I realize that I did things like that a lot in high school. For example, I was excited to be in the school musical, but when tryouts came I just couldn't do it. I want to work on being brave. Then, maybe, next time I'll have the courage to try something outside my comfort zone.

Comments: This example shows that the student backed out on something because she was afraid. Now it was something most people are afraid of, jumping off tall towers, but it took courage for her to admit the fear. Then, she pulled it back to the question about high school and how she didn't try drama, because she was afraid. Last, she states she would like to be braver and to try new things. This simple answer gave the interviewer a very deep view into the student. The interviewer can see how this student ticks a little more. Though she exposed a weakness, it came across as a strength, because she was working to do better next time.

Action Items

- Brainstorm 2-3 things you wanted to try in high school, but did not.
- Why? Not enough time? A fear? You just were not interested until later?
- Thinking about it now, is there something you learned about yourself?
- Organize your thoughts and form an answer.
- Practice your answer!

What is your favorite book?

This question is meant to bring out your critical thinking skills and see if you can articulate WHY a book is your favorite. Books can teach us things, bring out emotions, tell a story, spark our imaginations, or inspire us. What does your favorite book do for you? The interviewer does not care what your favorite book is instead he wants to know if the book inspires, teaches, or says something to you. And why is that important?

Start by figuring out what is your favorite book. What part or aspect of the book speaks to you? Why? What does it mean to you and why it is important? Has it taught or inspired you? Think through the answers to the previous questions and formulate a concise answer.

Example
What is your favorite book?

My favorite book is the "Princess Bride" by William Goldman. At the beginning of the book, the narrator explains how his grandfather would read to him while he was sick. The book had a little bit of everything; adventure, pirates, sword fighting, a giant, and true love. I like the Princess Bride, because it captures the essence of what I want my life to be like. I want to live everyday as an adventure and fill it with a little bit of everything. The book sparks my imagination and makes me believe that anything is possible. The beautiful girl is kidnapped and trades her life for that of her true love. The hero defies death to save his true love. The expert swordsman gets his revenge on the six-fingered man. They may only be characters in a book, but they remind me to look for the adventure in life and to continue fight on no matter what the odds are.

Comments: The speaker likes this particular book because it inspires her. She adds a few interesting details about the book while weaving in how the book affects her and her outlook on life. Pick your favorite book and dig down to find out why you like the book. Figure out how it has effected your life.

Action Items

- What is your favorite book?
- What about the book interests you? Why?
- What specific events in the book highlight your interest?
- Has the book taught you anything or inspired you to do something?
- Collect your thoughts and create an answer.
- Practice your answer!

Chapter 6
Other Common Questions

"Did you find the location okay? No?
I guess that explains why you were
over an hour late."

Below is a list of other common questions that could be asked of you in a college interview or possibly a scholarship interview. You will notice that many of the questions are a variation of the questions posed in the previous chapter. Many of the STAR stories you have already created can be reworded slightly and used to answer one or several of the questions below. No matter what the question is, remember that the interviewer is trying to understand why you are unique and how you would add value to the college. Tell a concise and interesting story about you and your life to answer. Avoid reciting any type of list for an answer. Avoid answering any question with a simple yes or no.

Ice Breaker Questions

Did you find the location okay?

How are you?

Are you having a good day so far?

Can you believe this weather?

See anything interesting on campus while you were here?

Questions about School

Describe your high school.

If there was one thing you could change about your high school, what would it be?

What does your high school do well?

Have you matured since you entered high school? How?

Which teachers have you connected with in high school and why?

In your eyes, what characteristics make a teacher great?

How do you hope college will be different from high school?

In creating your college list, what key characteristics are you looking for?

Given your expectations, why does "College X" interest you?

How do you see yourself interacting in and around "College X"?

What exactly do you hope to gain from your overall college experience?

What is your favorite subject in school and why?

Tell me about a meaningful academic class or project?

What is the most important thing you've learned in high school?

Give me an example of when you had too much to do. How did you resolve the conflicts in your schedule? How did you establish priorities for your efforts?

How do you manage and organize your time?

Have you won or been awarded any scholastic honors?

Questions about Friends/Family

Tell me about your friends.

How would you describe yourself to someone who did not know you?

Has your group of friends changed since you started high school? Why? How?

Which of your friends do you most admire and why?

Who makes up your family?

Describe what sorts of things you do as a family?

How is your family supporting you through this college search?

How would your friends describe you?

What are your best traits?

Which parent or other adult has the most influence on you?

What was your best source of information on "College X"?

Do you know anyone who has attended "College X"?

Questions about Extra-Curricular Activities

In what extracurricular activities did you participate in high school?

What achievements did you obtain from these activities?

In your extracurricular activities, what prominent leadership roles did you have?

Accomplishments?

Which of them give you the most satisfaction? Why?

What kind of periodicals do you read?

What was the name of the last book you read not in connection with schoolwork?

Have you at any time directed/organized people or participated in efforts designed to fill a community need?

Are you in a leadership position in any of your activities?

Describe for me any work you've done with or for civic/charitable groups.

Do you or have you ever had a part time job?

What is there about your job you like the most? Least?

How would your supervisor and co-worker describe you?

Is there anything else you want to add?

How do you define "success?"

What has been your proudest achievement so far?

What about you is unique?

What is the single most difficult task you have had to accomplish that you did not want to do?

What community service do you do? Why?

Who or what motivates you the most?

Tell me about a difficult experience that you have conquered. To what do you attribute this success?

Tell me about a situation in which you had to organize an activity?

Chapter 7

Tips and Tricks

"Are you sure you tried hard enough to be on time?"

1) Confirm the time and place with your interviewer or consult the written instructions given. Send any requested information on time or as early as possible. Follow all instructions given in interview guidance.

2) Arrive ten to fifteen minutes early. Have a few minutes by yourself to be quiet and think about what you want to say. Stay away from others and focus on how you want to express yourself. Review your Most Common Questions with your associated STAR stories and review your resume. If you spent sufficient time on your STAR stories you will already be well organized and they should encompass what is on your resume. It is in your best interest to formulate everything you can into a STAR story and PRACTICE. The more you practice to a mirror, friends, or family, the more confident you will be. Take a deep breath before entering the room. Clear your mind from worries. You are ready!

3) Wear professional clothing. Guys, this includes a tie and khakis at least. Black slacks or a suit is fine too. You want to be clean shaven and wear nice shoes. Wear your best clothing. Ladies, black pants or a skirt, a nice top, black pumps (or something similar), minimal make-up, and well-groomed hair. Remember, you are not going to a club. You are not trying to look hot. You are trying to look professional. If you are confused you can ask an adult who you think acts and

looks professional their opinion on your wardrobe. If there is a suggested wardrobe given in your interview instructions, follow the advice/guidelines.

4) Eye contact. You must practice good eye contact during an interview. You do not want to stare intently though. In fact, if you are too intense it begins to feel awkward. You want to be able to look at those interviewing you most of the time, but you can look up, down or around as you speak. But you need to be conscious of your audience and look at them. With a one-on-one interview act like you are having a conversion with a friend and look them in the eye.

In a group setting with a panel of people, several people will take turns asking you questions. Begin answering your question to the person who asked the question for about ten to fifteen seconds. Then, as you continue your answer start to look around the room and make eye contact with the rest of the people in the panel. Make them feel part of the conversation. Do not just focus on the one who asked you the question. All the people in the panel are evaluating you. They need to know that you are talking to each person and not just the one that asked the question. So, start with the person who asked the question and then look around the room at each person. Do not dart back and forth. Look at someone, make eye contact for a few seconds and then move on to the next person. Always come back to who initially asked you the question to finish up.

5) Think about the question. When someone asks you a question you can think about it for a few seconds. Three or four seconds may seem like an eternity in your mind but do not panic. A few seconds to the interviewer is not going to look awkward. Just think for a few seconds, organize your thoughts, and then answer appropriately. If you have written and practiced your STAR stories it should be very simple to answer. Well written STAR stories can be slightly changed to accommodate the flavor of the question. Just filter through which one seems the most appropriate, adjust it slightly, and then start your answer.

But let's say you panic. You wrote your stories out, but you are drawing a blank on question number one. A ten to fifteen seconds pause will seem a little awkward. To give yourself a few more seconds to think you can clarify the question. That is an appropriate way to give yourself a little bit of time and not seem awkward when answering the question.

For example, question one is, "Tell me about yourself." Nothing comes to mind. You need to stall so you can clear your head and think. So you ask, "Are you more interested in my school or extracurricular activities?" Okay not the best respond to a question, but it will give you time to think. The interviewer answers, "school activities." Okay, school, you think. I can do school. "I am involved with track, cross country,....."

6) Add real excitement and emotion to your stories. Do not force emotion, but avoid sounding like your most boring teacher at school. Pay attention in class and see which teachers seem the most interesting. They probably are good at putting emotion and interest into their voices. Also, PRACTICE those STAR stories. I know I am foot stomping the STAR stories and there is a reason. The more you practice them, the more confidence you will have as you talk. This will make you appear natural and able to engage your audience.

Additionally, you want to use your hands when you talk. Not too much, but use your hands for emphasis. You do not want to seem stiff, very uncomfortable or very nervous. Keeping your hands glued to your lap will make you appear this way. The best way to help yourself is to practice with somebody. Practice with a friend, with your parents, with your stuffed animals, or a mirror. Other than the stuffed animals, you can get feedback if your speech and hand gestures seem natural. If you are like me, and have a tendency to play with a pen or other object when nervous, keep the pen or object away from yourself during the interview.

85

7) Do not ramble or answer any question with a list. Example, if they ask, "What activities you are involved in?" A list may seem an appropriate way to answer and in a way it is. Offer three or four activities and then offer a short example or STAR story. Something like this, "I am Captain of my football team, I am vice President of the Senior Class, I play basketball, and I am involved in volunteering through my church. I really enjoy my volunteering activities. My favorite activity was cleaning a very nice older woman's home. Her husband had died and she had trouble keeping the house up so our church group had come to help her. I got talking with her while cleaning and offered to come back and mow her lawn. She had the biggest smile and it made me feel really good about helping her."

Now, if I had answered the question with a list of ten things what would the panel have learned about me? Nothing that my resume had not already told them. But the short story gave them a lot more about me than a list. Cleaning someone's house or mowing a lawn is not a major volunteer effort or even an amazing effort. But that little story will stick with the interviewer. Lists are hard to remember, but stories last in our minds. Think about the little things you like or enjoy about your activities. I bet there is a story behind why you like or enjoy it.

8) Be short and concise. The STAR stories are (I can't emphasize STAR stories enough) going to help you in this tip. They help because you wrote them to be concise and you have practiced them. Follow the STAR story format to tell what is really important and you will stay on task.

9) Be real and avoid jokes. Humor is one of those things that is hard to judge. Some things are funny to some people and some things are not funny to others. Natural humor as you talk or tell a funny story that happened to you is okay, but avoid outright jokes. They usually fall flat and could even offend someone. Be yourself and do not go out of your way to make people laugh.

10) Read your audience. The best way to do this is to practice and have confidence. If your audience looks a little glazed over or are looking sleepy, maybe you are going on too long. You could be rambling or could have given them a long list of things that they could not process. Read your audience's reaction and adjust. Think about your answers and think about the previous interview tips. Make adjustments and reengage with your panel. This is a fairly advanced tip and hard to accomplish, but can be done if you practice.

Also, connecting a previous comment or experience the interviewer has shared is an excellent way to impress interviewers. For example, let's say your interviewer introduced himself and says that he graduated from the college and was a history major. History happens to be one of your possible majors. When you talk about your possible majors reference his comment about being a history major and that you, as well, may consider that. It will show him that you were paying attention to his introduction. Also, at the end of the interview you could ask what he liked most about being a history major.

11) I have already emphasized this a few times, but know something about the college you are interviewing with. You would be surprised how many students do not know anything about the college they are interviewing with. This is a huge, huge red flag for those interviewing you. It announces in neon lights that you really do not want to attend the college and you are wasting the interviewer's time. This is unacceptable in today's day and age. Get on the internet, read up on the websites, Facebook page and blogs, and watch some college sponsored YouTube videos. It will take you thirty minutes to an hour. Well worth the time investment.

12) What to answer for the "What can I tell you about our college?" question. There is almost always time at the end for you to ask questions. Try to avoid questions that you could easily look up online. Questions like, "when is the application

deadline?" or when will you be letting students know if they were accepted?" Instead ask an insightful question about the college. You did some research, so what would you like to know? You saw that there are research opportunities at the school. A good question might be, "I am interested in doing research as an undergraduate. Who would I talk to on campus about looking into those opportunities further?" Or maybe a question like this, "I saw that there is a study abroad program. What is the most valuable thing that students get out of the experience?" Or if you know the interviewer graduated from the college, you can ask, "As a graduate what do you think is the best activity to participate in while attending "College X?"

13) Schedule your college interviews wisely. Even if you are practicing your STAR stories for your friends or parents, you will get better with each interview. Try to schedule your interviews with your top choices last. This will give you the most time to practice and be most comfortable for your number one choice.

14) Do not look at the clock. If you have been practicing your STAR stories your answers will be informative and concise. If the interviewer looks at their watch do not worry. Interviews are usually scheduled back-to-back so the interviewer has a schedule to keep.

15) Be considerate and thankful to anyone who interviews you. Send a thank-you note. If you found something helpful or you had a shared experience mention it briefly. Most of all make sure to express your interest in the school and your gratitude for the time the interviewer took to meet with you.

LAST: I have said this over and over but it is probably the most important. Practice, practice, practice, practice! Here is the way I suggest to do this. Start with your STAR stories, write them out. Read them over and over again, memorize them, and then do a mock interview in front of a mirror. Ask family and friends to interview you and ask them for feedback. Really ask them for what you could have done better and what you can do to improve either your stories or presentation. When you interview with your parents or your friends, use your STAR stories to tell them something they may not even know about you. Try and tell them something new and interesting.

Chapter 8
Last But Not Least

Your future awaits.
Pick a door.

GOOD LUCK!!!!

You have worked hard to improve your interview skills. I know the exercises and practice are time consuming, but it is worth it. Interviewing for college is no different than interviewing for a scholarship, internship, job, or anything else. You can pull this book out for any interview. The methodology will be the same. Find out about the company/position/organization. Then, put yourself in the shoes of the person/company interviewing you, and figure out what they are interested in. Then, review the STAR Stories section. Create several STAR stories that will address their concerns/interests. PRACTICE!!! And you will be ready to dazzle any interviewer with your skills, confidence, and pose!

Don't forget to look for my book <u>I Can Write An Extraordinary College Essay</u> on Amazon. It teaches techniques similar to this book and will help you write essay that will stand out from the crowd.

I hoped you enjoyed this book. I love helping students improve their interview skills. Please take a second to give it a great review on Amazon. Thanks!

35030236R00054

Made in the USA
Middletown, DE
16 September 2016